DINOSAURS

D1396187

DINOSAURS

by David Lambert
Illustrated by Ross Wardle

Willowisp Press

Published in 1985 by Willowisp Press, Inc.
401 E. Wilson Bridge Road, Worthington, Ohio 43085

This Book Fair Edition published by arrangement with
Granada Publishing Limited
London, England

Copyright ©Granada
American Text Copyright ©1985 by Willowisp Press, Inc.

ISBN 0-87406-054-2

Printed and bound in Italy by
New Interlitho, Milan

10 9 8 7 6 5 4 3 2 1

Granada ®
Granada Publishing ®

Contents

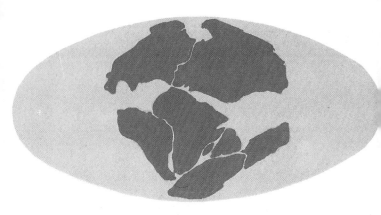

The Triassic Period
The world probably looked like this during the Triassic Period (225-193 million years ago). All the lands had been joined in one huge continent called Pangaea. This was breaking up. But the first dinosaurs could wander across Pangaea from one end to the other.

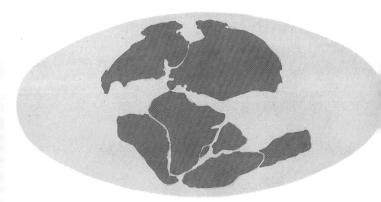

The Jurassic Period
During the Jurassic Period (193-135 million years ago), the northern and southern continents were separating. But land bridges let the dinosaurs wander north and south.

The Age of Dinosaurs

Long before the first man, larger animals than any that are found today roamed the Earth. We call these animals dinosaurs, or "terrible lizards." But they were not lizards. And they were unlike any other reptiles now alive. Some of the dinosaurs ate plants and some ate flesh.

For 140 million years, dinosaurs ruled the land. The Age of Dinosaurs, called the Mesozoic Era, began around 225 million years ago. It ended 65 million years ago. It is divided into three periods — the Triassic, Jurassic, and Cretaceous.

The maps on these pages show how dinosaurs spread around the world.

The Cretaceous Period
In the Cretaceous Period (135-65 million years ago) oceans separated most of the land masses. Dinosaurs could not travel easily from one continent to another.

At the start of the Mesozoic Era, the world was very different from today. There were no grasses or flowering plants of any kind. Ferns, tree-ferns, horsetails, and palmlike trees or cycads thrived on marshy land. Evergreen or needle-leafed trees grew on dry ground. In that Triassic period, large parts of the world were barren desert.

The Jurassic period was wetter and warmer. Large forests grew.

During the Cretaceous period much of the land cooled down. Flowering plants multiplied. The first trees to shed their leaves in winter began to spread.

The dinosaurs shared the land with many different kinds of reptiles. There were lizards, tortoises, and crocodiles unlike those today. Prior to dinosaurs, there had been large mammallike reptiles. They had died out long before the first dinosaurs appeared. This left no land animals large enough or strong enough to threaten or fight the dinosaurs. The early mammals were tiny and timid.

Some plants and creatures living early in the Mesozoic Era were the turtlelike Henodus (bottom left), Protosuchus (bottom right) and behind them Euparkeria (left) and Coelophysis (right).

Masters of the Land

Dinosaurs can be traced back through the ages to a group of fish. Fish were the first animals to have backbones. They developed into early amphibians. These creatures could live and breathe on land. But they entered water to moisten their skin and to lay their eggs.

After amphibians came reptiles. These creatures had scaly skins and laid waterproof eggs. They were able to live and breed on land.

The archosaurs, or "ruling reptiles," had longer, straighter legs than the other reptiles. The dinosaurs belonged to this group.

Some people think dinosaurs were warm-blooded and more active than ordinary cold-blooded reptiles. Nobody knows for sure.

Euparkeria, an early archosaur, was an ancestor of many of the dinosaurs.

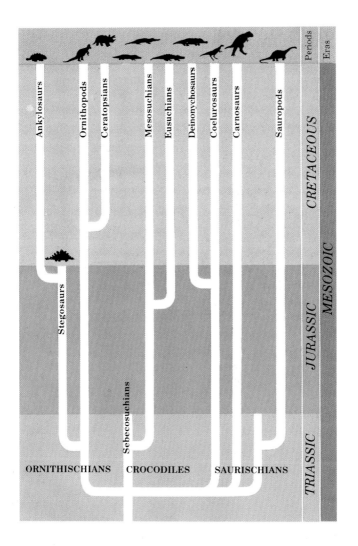

The family tree shows the archosaurs. Only the crocodiles are alive today. The dinosaurs were divided into two groups—the ornithischians and saurischians.

11

Life in Air and Water

Dinosaurs ruled the land. Other beasts became masters of the sea and air.

Two groups of large reptiles lived entirely in the sea. They had flippers in place of legs. They could paddle, but they could not walk.

Ichthyosaurs means "fish lizards." They looked and moved very much like modern dolphins. They hunted fish and could swim faster than any other animal.

Plesiosaurs, meaning "near lizard," had large bodies and short tails. They used flat flippers to swim underwater. They used the same rowing action as penguins or turtles. Long-necked plesiosaurs caught fish near the surface.

An ichthyosaur, a long-necked plesiosaur and a pterosaur.

Some ichthyosaurs and the plesiosaur Elasmosaurus grew up to 33 ft (10 m) long.

Pteranodon's spread wings were about 23 ft (7 m) wide. This flimsy gliderlike creature weighed only one quarter as much as a man.

The short-necked plesiosaurs, called pliosaurs, dived to hunt for food. But all the sea reptiles had to come up to the surface to breathe.

Pterosaurs or "winged lizards" were lightweight beasts with hollow bones. Leathery batlike membranes were supported by one long, bony finger. They glided through the air.

Little *Pterodactylus* was the size of a small bird. But *Quetzalcoatlus* had wings 46 feet (14 meters) across. Pterosaurs had short legs.

Giant Creatures

Imagine a giant scaly beast with a body the size of an elephant, a giraffe's neck, and a tail as long and partly as thick as a telegraph pole. Such beasts roamed the warm, damp forests of the Mesozoic Era.

Sauropods means "lizard feet." They had five toes like lizards. They belonged to the saurischian or "lizard-hipped" dinosaurs. Sauropods were the largest dinosaurs and the largest land animals that ever lived.

Each sauropod had four legs as large as tree trunks. Despite its size, its backbone was hollow

and lightweight. Muscles fixed to its bones swung the neck and tail up and down, from side to side.

A sauropod had a head larger than a horse. It had a smaller brain for its size than any other backboned beast that has ever lived.

From the remains of jaws, scientists know sauropods ate only plants. They were probably harmless. They lived in much the same way as elephants do today, spending most of the time browsing peacefully. Their size alone would have protected them from enemies.

A herd of Barosaurus plods through a tropical forest in North America or East Africa about 140 million years ago.

How Sauropods Evolved

About 225 million years ago, sauropods and all other dinosaurs came from small, sprawling, lizardlike creatures. A few million years later, these animals developed into larger beasts. They lived in lakes and rivers.

Over the years, bodies changed in ways that helped the creatures to swim. A large, powerful tail grew. Limbs grew down instead of sideways. They moved from the hips and shoulders, no longer from the knees and elbows. The beasts could move powerfully against the water with their limbs. They could also take long strides when they walked on land.

Ticinosuchus was a reptile 7-9 ft (2-3 m) long. Its back legs were longer than its front legs but it walked on all fours. It lived in what is now Switzerland and other places.

Thecodontosaurus measured 7-9 ft (2-3 m). It had small, saw-edged teeth. It may have been the first kind of dinosaur to feed on plants, as well as insects and other creatures. It lived in Europe.

The early archosaurs lived mostly on the land. One was *Euparkeria*. Another was *Ticinosuchus*. It looked like a long-legged crocodile.

Ticinosuchus was a sharp-toothed flesh-eater. Four-legged animals with blunter teeth and a taste for leaves may have come from it. They included the early creature *Thecodontosaurus*.

Such beasts were no longer than *Ticinosuchus*. Their descendant, *Plateosaurus,* was a plant-eater twice as long as the *Ticinosuchus*. Later came the even longer *Melanorosaurus*.

These animals and others led directly to the gigantic sauropods.

Plateosaurus was about 20 ft (6 m) long. It could raise its neck as high as 9 ft (3 m) to eat the leaves growing from the tops of palmlike trees. It lived in Europe.

The sauropods were divided into two main groups — the camarasaurids and the atlantosaurids.

The Camarasaurids

The hollow chambers in the backbone earned these dinosaurs the name *Camarasaurus*. It means "chambered lizard." *Camarasaurus* was about 35 feet (10 meters) long. But its relative, *Cetiosaurus*, meaning "whale lizard," measured up to 59 feet (18 meters).

Brachiosaurus or "arm lizard" was among the largest and the heaviest of the dinosaurs. This creature had front legs longer than its hind legs. The head was short with nostrils near the front. Dozens of short, blunt, strong teeth rimmed the jaws. Some creatures weighed up to 80 tons.

Pieces of an even larger monster have been discovered in North America. It has been nicknamed *Supersaurus*. It may have weighed over 100 tons. If so, it was the heaviest land animal that ever lived.

The Atlantosaurids

These sauropods had nostrils high on the head between the eyes. Their weak teeth were found only in front of the jaws. The group is named after *Atlantosaurus,* a giant in Greek myth. It measured 82 feet (25 meters) from head to tail.

Barosaurus and *Diplodocus,* which means "double beam," belonged to this group. The name *Diplodocus* describes the "skids" on its tailbones. These helped to guard blood vessels in the tail if it dragged on the ground. *Diplodocus* was the longest of all dinosaurs. It measured 85 feet (26 meters).

Diplodocus (left) could rear on its long hind legs, using its tail as a prop. Brachiosaurus (right) had longer front legs than back legs. It was shorter, but far heavier than Diplodocus. Both could raise their long necks very high.

The Benefits of Being Big

Sauropods seemed to have had bodies which were much too big to work efficiently. But their huge size had advantages. Most flesh-eating animals would not attack. Also, their great cold-blooded bodies cooled down slowly at night. This helped to keep their bodies warm.

Their great size may have been needed to digest food. Scientists believe that a large sauropod ate half a ton of plant food every day. But many dinosaurs only had peglike teeth. They were not able to grind up all this food. Swallowed stones in the stomach may have ground the food instead. The stomach had to be very large.

None of these creatures survived into the Cretaceous period or left descendants. Their size probably protected the adults. But the young animals were vulnerable to carnosaurs (meat-eaters).

Land or Water Animals?

People once thought that sauropods only ate soft water plants. People argued that the giants were very heavy. They must have spent their lives buoyed up by water. Their long necks were supposed to help them breathe as they waded in deep lakes.

Tracks found show that some sauropods could swim. But scientists now know their strong, large legs could support their weight on land.

Tracks also show that dinosaurs roamed in herds like huge elephants. They probably used their long necks to reach treetop leaves like giraffes do today.

Above: A full-grown and a young Camarasaurus. Baby sauropods were born from big, almost round, eggs which were hatched by the heat of the sun. Scientists do not know if dinosaur parents looked after their young or if they had to fend for themselves.

Right: This sauropod skull was light for its size because of the large gaps between the bony struts. The weak peglike teeth were not very well suited for grinding leaves.

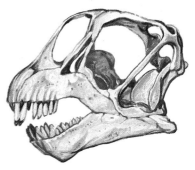

21

The Flesh-Eaters

Long ago flesh-eating dinosaurs preyed on the plant-eating dinosaurs. There were more plant-eaters than flesh-eaters, just as there are today. But the flesh-eaters must have been extremely fierce.

Tyrannosaurus rex, "king of the tyrant lizards," was perhaps the largest, most terrible of all meat-eating dinosaurs. It measured 46 feet (14 meters) from snout to tail and was heavier than an African bull elephant. It walked on huge hind legs. Its toes were tipped with long sharp claws.

A Tyrannosaurus attacks an Alamosaurus. These dinosaurs lived in North America about 70 million years ago.

The creature's jaw could open three feet wide. Just as terrifying were the creature's teeth. Rows of six-inch, double-edged fangs rimmed jaws that could tear flesh from its helpless victims. Only the monster's arms seemed too short and weak to do much damage.

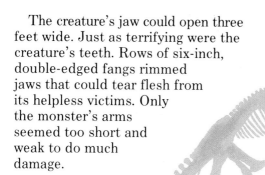

The skeleton of Tyrannosaurus

The Beast-Footed Dinosaurs

All flesh-eating creatures also belonged to the group of lizard-hipped dinosaurs, like the sauropods. The sauropods walked on four legs and had rounded feet like an elephant's.

The flesh-eaters walked on two legs. They had long toes and claws. Their feet gave them the speed a hunter needs and fearful weapons for holding, kicking, and clawing.

Flesh-eating dinosaurs are called theropods. This means "beast feet."

How Theropods Began

Theropods came from reptile ancestors like little *Euparkeria*. One of the earliest theropods was *Coelophysis*. This lively and quick dinosaur ran fast on its long hind legs. It grasped its prey in its "hands."

Coelophysis roamed North America. *Ornithosuchus* lived in what is now Scotland. Both were about as long as a small car and ran on hind legs,

balanced by the tail. *Ornithosuchus* was heavier than *Coelophysis*.

Experts are not sure if *Ornithosuchus* was a dinosaur. They believe early dinosaurs like it developed into the largest and fiercest flesh-eating dinosaurs. Beasts like *Coelophysis* developed into a separate group of hunters which were much smaller, lighter, and more agile.

Coelophysis (left) and Ornithosuchus
were both between 8-10 ft (2.5 m — 3 m)
long. Ornithosuchus weighed 110 lbs
(50 kg) and was built to hunt larger prey
than Coelophysis could kill. They
would not have preyed on each other.

Carnosaur Killers

Carnosaurs were the big hunters in the Age of Dinosaurs. Their name means "flesh lizards." The first main group to arise were the megalosaurs or "large lizards."

Megalosaurus measured 42 feet (6 meters). It walked on huge, powerful hind legs. It held its head forward, balanced by its long, heavy tail. This

The megalosaur Ceratosaurus had a bony horn on its nose.

Megalosaurus had solid, thick leg bones. They had to be big and strong to bear its weight.

Tyrannosaurus had a skull so huge that a man's head could fit inside one eye socket. Holes in the skull make it lighter than it looks.

dinosaur may have gripped plant-eating dinosaurs with its clawed hands. Then it may have slashed them to death with the great claws on its hind legs. It would then have used its sharp, curved fangs and saw-edged teeth to bite off mouthfuls of flesh.

Beasts like *Megalosaurus* had thin skulls. Thick bone guarded the eyes.

Among the largest megalosaurs was *Allosaurus* or "leaping lizard." *Allosaurus* was as long as a bus and weighed two tons. Footprints discovered in rocks showed that an *Allosaurus* chased a sauropod. *Allosaurus* may have killed plant-eating dinosaurs 40 times as heavy as itself.

The Terrible Tyrannosaurids

Tyrannosaurids were larger than the largest megalosaurs. *Tyrannosaurus* and *Albertosaurus* lived in North America. *Tarbosaurus* roamed east Asia. *Genyodectes* was at home in South America. They all appeared during the Cretaceous period.

Surprisingly, tyrannosaurids may have been cold-blooded. Meat equal to one sauropod would have fed a 10-ton tyrannosaurid for two years.

Birdlike Dinosaurs

Coelurosaurs were much smaller hunters than their closest relatives, the carnosaurs. Their bones were thin and hollow instead of thick and solid like those of carnosaurs. They could run very fast on their long, slim hind legs.

A running coelurosaur held its long neck stretched forward and was balanced by its long, scaly tail. It probably dashed in between bushes and used its clawed fingers to seize small beasts, such as lizards and early mammals.

Two Coelurus feed on the huge carcass of a dead sauropod. Their "hands" help them to tear off flesh. These coelurosaurs probably ate carnosaurs' leftovers just as hyenas share in a lion's kill today.

Compsognathus and Archaeopteryx, the first known bird, lived in Germany 150 million years ago. Birds may have come from small, warm-blooded dinosaurs. Their scales frayed and developed into feathers that helped to keep them warm.

Coelurosaurs also probably fed on the remains of large, dead beasts.

One of the first coelurosaurs was *Coelophysis.* Later kinds included *Coelurus,* which is also known as *Ornitholestes.* It was longer than a man, but not as heavy.

Compsognathus was a coelurosaur which was a little larger than a modern chicken. Except for its teeth, arms, bony tail, and scaly skin, it looked like a bird.

It is possible that modern birds came from dinosaurs like this. Some scientists think, however, that the fossil of *Compsognathus* was not that of a full-grown animal.

An Ornithomimus raids a nest. Others are chased by a Torosaurus.

Bird Mimics

Around 135 million years ago, at the beginning of the Cretaceous period, a new group of coelurosaurs appeared. Scientists call this unusual family the Ornithomimidae. They included *Ornithomimus* or "bird mimic" and *Struthiomimus* or "ostrich mimic" from North America.

These coelurosaurs had a toothless, horny beak. The head joined the neck at the same angle as a bird's. They looked very much like some of today's big, long-legged flightless birds.

Struthiomimus stood slightly taller than an ostrich. Like the ostriches, bird mimics had long, light leg bones built for sprinting at up to 50 miles (80 kilometers) an hour. The dinosaur *Dromiceiomimus* probably ran even faster. Bird mimics must have been warm-blooded to reach such speeds.

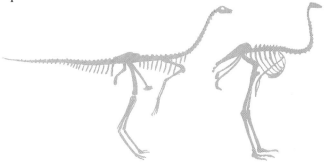

The skeletons of an ostrich dinosaur (left) and an ostrich are much alike. Both have long legs that end in long toes. Ostrich dinosaurs no doubt sprinted just like ostriches.

Bird mimics were different from true birds. They had arms, not wings, and tough skin instead of feathers. The tail was long and thin like a lizard's.

Egg-Stealers?

How bird mimics used their beaks and claws for feedings is not known. One clue, though, was discovered upon finding an *Oviraptor* or "egg stealer." It was found dead on a nest of eggs laid by another dinosaur. *Oviraptor* and other bird mimics probably uncovered dinosaur eggs with their claws. Then they sucked the eggs dry.

Terrible Claws

Coelurosaurs and carnosaurs produced several strange flesh-eaters during the Cretaceous period.

Among the stranger carnosaurs was *Spinosaurus.* It lived in Egypt. It was 39 feet (12 meters) long. It had long front legs and walked on all fours, unlike most carnosaurs.

From its backbone grew bony spikes that held up a tall, skin-covered "sail." This sail could have controlled body temperature. *Spinosaurus* warmed up quickly with its sail broadside to the sun. With its tail edge facing toward the sun, it cooled down.

From the coelurosaurs came a group of small, savage killers called deinonychosaurs. This means "terrible claws."

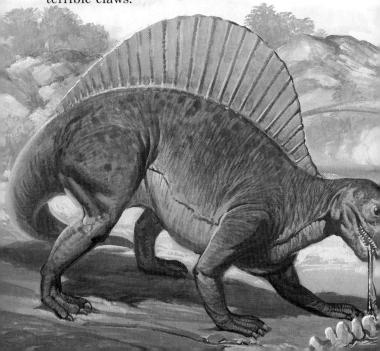

Deinonychus ran very fast on long hind legs. Scientists believe deinonychosaurs hunted in packs and killed dinosaurs far larger than themselves. To attack, it may have seized an enemy with the claws on its long arms. Then it stood on one leg and slashed with the huge claw on its second toe. Its long, stiff tail helped it keep its balance.

They lived in North America and Asia.

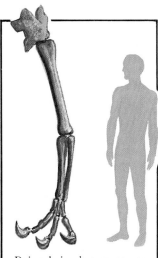

Deinocheirus's arm was as long as a man's and had a "terrible claw" at the end.

Spinosaurus was a four-legged carnosaur. On its back was a sail that served as a radiator, keeping it at the right temperature. In the background is Deinonychus, a small killer that may have been feared more than Tyrannosaurus.

33

Biped Browsers

Ornithischian or "bird-hipped" dinosaurs earned their name from the shape of their hipbones. All the bird-hipped dinosaurs were plant eaters.

Some ornithischians walked on two legs and some walked on four. Those that walked on two legs are called ornithopods. This means "bird feet."

Iguanodon is probably the best known of all two-legged bird-hipped dinosaurs. It measured up to 30 feet (9 meters). It was as heavy as an elephant. Its flat teeth and blunt claws show that it was a harmless plant-eater. *Iguanodon* walked on its hind legs.

About 100 million years ago *Iguanodon,* or its close relatives, lived as far apart as northern Europe and Australia. Its main enemies were the fierce megalosaurs.

Megalosaurs may have chased a whole *Iguanodon* herd over a cliff. Miners once came across 31 of the creatures' skeltons lying together.

One Iguanodon eats while others run away from a Megalosaurus.

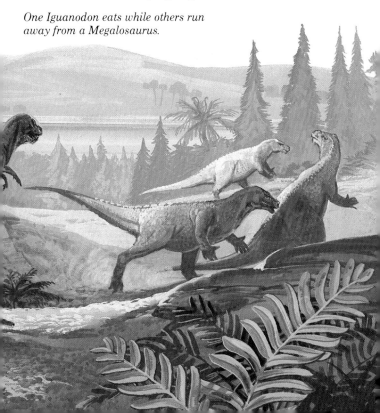

Bird-Hipped Bipeds

Iguanodon sprang from bird-hipped bipeds the size of a large lizard. One bird-hipped biped was *Heterodontosaurus*. It means roughly "lizard with different teeth." The beast had some sharp cutting teeth and other teeth with flattish tops. They were more like a mammal's teeth than a reptile's.

Heterodontosaurus also had cheek pouches to store food as it chewed. These plant-eaters were usually about 4-5 feet (1-1.5 meters) long. They were found mainly in what is now Africa.

Two early bird-hipped bipeds are Lesothosaurus (in the foreground) and Heterodontosaurus.

Hypsilophodon was small and agile. People used to think this plant-eater perched on branches. Now they believe it lived on the ground and ran fast enough to escape enemies.

Another of the early bird-hipped bipeds was *Lesothosaurus*. It had sharp teeth. But its lower jaw ended in a horny beak. This would have helped it to chop off leaves and twigs. *Lesothosaurus* lived in the southern part of Africa.

The larger bird-footed dinosaurs, like *Iguanodon*, came from beasts like *Heterodontosaurus* and *Lesothosaurus*. All of them had jaws which were designed for cropping leaves and grinding them.

Hypsilophodonts were one group that changed very little as the Mesozoic wore on. *Hypsilophodon* was almost as long as a man. It was speedy and slender. It could probably sprint and leap like today's gazelles.

Iguanodonts

Camptosaurus stood nearly 16 ft (5 m) tall and most herds probably grazed on all fours. The huge animal measured up to 23 ft (7 m) and weighed nearly 4 tons.

Iguanodonts mean "iguana teeth." They get their name from the shape of their teeth which were like those of a huge iguana lizard. These bird-footed dinosaurs were very large. *Camptosaurus* and *Iguanodon* each weighed several tons.

Iguanodonts had a long tongue that pulled leaves into the mouth. They did not have front upper teeth. To chop off a mouthful of leaves they pressed the leaves between a hard upper pad and the horny beak at the tip of the lower jaw. Rows of grinding teeth at the back of the jaws ground the leaves to pulp. Meanwhile cheek pouches held more leaves waiting to be chewed.

Iguanodonts could breathe while they ate, unlike ordinary reptiles. This made it possible for them to chew food slowly.

Camptosaurus and *Iguanodon* had hooves on all four limbs. But they walked mainly on their hind legs. *Camptosaurus* lived much earlier than *Iguanodon*.

Iguanodon could stab enemies with its spiky thumbs, but had no other really good means of defense. This iguanodont was larger than Camptosaurus and lived much later.

Bone-Headed Dinosaurs

In northern lands, toward the end of the Mesozoic Era, a strange new group of bird-footed dinosaurs developed.

First came a turkey-sized dinosaur, *Yaverlandia.* It had a long, stiff tail and bony bumps above its eyes. *Yaverlandia* lived in southern England.

Later, larger dinosaurs with thicker skulls developed. One was the man-sized *Stegoceras.* It had a brain as small as a hen's egg. Yet the skull around it was up to five times thicker than a man's. *Stegoceras* lived in Canada and China.

The largest and last bone-headed dinosaur was North America's *Pachycephalosaurus.* Its name means "thick-headed lizard."

Pachycephalosaurus had a very thick skull. It was three times longer and four times thicker than *Stegoceras's* skull. Bony knobs reinforced the front and back.

Experts believe the thick skulls protected the creature's brains. Rival males butted one another in battles to win females in the same way that rival stags fight with their antlers today.

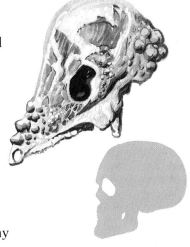

Pachycephalosaurus used its thick skull as a weapon. The skull was 20 times thicker than a man's.

Duckbilled Dinosaurs

Among the last and most successful of the dinosaurs were Hadrosaurs, meaning "big lizards." Scientists have found more remains of Hadrosaurs than of any other dinosaur. Hadrosaurs resembled their ancestors, the iguanodonts.

Hadrosaurs measured up to 33 feet (10 meters). They probably weighed just over three tons, less than *Iguanodon*. They are often called duckbilled dinosaurs, after their ducklike beaks. But their jaws held rows of grinding teeth. Some species had 2,000 teeth.

A feeding group of duckbilled Corythosaurus with "helmets" that doubled the height of the head. One dinosaur keeps watch for carnosaurs.

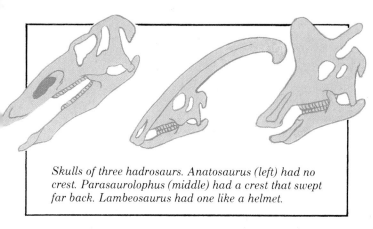

Skulls of three hadrosaurs. Anatosaurus (left) had no crest. Parasaurolophus (middle) had a crest that swept far back. Lambeosaurus had one like a helmet.

As old teeth fell out, new ones grew to take their place. These grinding teeth helped duckbills chew needlelike leaves and other tough plant foods. Remains of these leaves were actually found in the body of one dead duckbilled dinosaur.

This proved that duckbills did not feed on soft water plants. But they probably swam using their flattened tails and webbed fingers. Swimming or running was their only defense. But they had keen ears and eyes to warn them of approaching danger.

Mysterious Crests

The strangest thing about some duckbills was the bony crest that sprouted from the head. There were about one dozen kinds of duckbills with differently shaped crests.

What purpose the bony crests served is a mystery. They would have been of little use in protecting the animals. They may have heightened their sense of smell. This would have enabled the duckbills to pick up the scent of an enemy in the distance.

Living Battle Tanks

Three groups of four-legged bird-hipped dinosaurs developed. These quadrupeds had horny beaks for eating plants. But unlike their two-legged cousins, most were probably too slow to run away from danger. They depended on built-in body armor for defense.

The first group was the stegosaurs or "plated lizards." They had bony plates which jutted from their backs, like *Stegosaurus*.

Rival Stegosaurus males threaten one another. In the background a female seems to take no notice as she munches leaves.

Stegosaurus was as long as two full-size cars. It stood room high. *Stegosaurus* weighed up to two tons, slightly less than a full-grown hippopotamus.

The tall bony plates on its back jutted upward. These plates probably released unwanted body heat.

Stegosaurus's brain was only the size of a walnut. Low down in its backbone was a hollow space. This space probably held a special tissue which helped feed energy to the dinosaur's back legs.

Plated Dinosaurs

Over 150 million years ago creatures like *Stegosaurus* roamed lush forests in North America and Europe. These armored beasts took millions of years of gradual change to develop.

The first known plated dinosaur was the creature *Scelidosaurus*. It lived in southern England 190 million years ago. For protection rows of low bony studs ran down the creature's back. Any carnosaur that tried to bite it risked having its teeth snapped off.

Scelidosaurus was a low-slung dinosaur about 13 ft (4 m) long, with a small head and weak jaws. Sometimes it may have walked on its hind legs. Its limbs ended in claws, not hooves like those of later stegosaurs.

Chialingosaurus was a plated dinosaur from the area of China. Small plates were shaped like spines. *Lexovisaurus*, another plated dinosaur, was protected by both flat plates and spines.

One of the spiniest of all the plated dinosaurs was *Kentrosaurus*. This plated dinosaur lived in eastern Africa at the same time as *Stegosaurus*.

Kentrosaurus's neck and back were well protected. Its spiked tail was probably capable of giving a death-blow. But the animal would have lacked speed. While turning to strike an enemy with its tail, its unprotected sides would have been vulnerable to attack. If it reared up on its hind legs to feed, its unplated underparts would have been unprotected.

Two rows of bony plates and spikes guarded Kentrosaurus's neck, back, and tail. Kentrosaurus lived at the same time as Stegosaurus. It was only half as long as its American cousin.

All plated dinosaurs died out before the end of the Jurassic period about 135 million years ago. Probably their defenses were not good enough to fend off the huge carnosaurs that preyed on them.

Armored Dinosaurs

When the plated dinosaurs died out armored descendants followed. This second group was able to cope with the flesh-eaters. Their bodies were low-slung. They could drop down to the ground when danger threatened. These armored dinosaurs may even have been able to roll up like armadillos do today.

One early armored dinosaur was *Acanthopholis.* This beast was as long as a small car. Short spines guarded its shoulders. Flat, hinged plates protected the back and tail. *Polacanthus* was larger and spikier. Both lived in Europe 115 million years ago.

"Stiff Lizards"

Armor-plated dinosaurs with curved stiff ribs were named ankylosaurs. This means "stiff lizards." Later kinds of ankylosaurs had plates and spikes that formed a kind of shell.

The best protected was *Euoplocephalus* (once called *Ankylosaurus).* A blanket of bony plates covered its back from head to tail. These plates ended in a large bony club. *Euplocephalus* means "armored-head." It was heavy and long like a large rhinoceros.

Even harder to attack was *Scolosaurus.* Its name means "thorn lizard." This creature looked like a spiky tortoise the size of a hippopotomus. Carnosaurs could easily kill such beasts. They only had to tip them over to claw their soft bellies.

Scientists have found the remains of ankylosaurs lying on their backs. The creatures may have drowned and not been attacked. Perhaps they fell in prehistoric rivers and drifted onto sandbanks upside down.

Polacanthus was an armor-plated beast about 16 ft (5 m) long. Its neck, shoulders, and tail were protected by spines. Bony knobs protected its lower back. This dinosaur roamed southern England.

Euoplocephalus measured 16 ft (5 m) and weighed about 3 tons. It was protected by bony plates set in its skin.

Scolosaurus weighed 3.5 tons. Bony spikes protected its back. Its tail was a spiky club.

Horned Dinosaurs

Horned dinosaurs were the third group of armored dinosaurs. Scientists call them ceratopsians. This means "horned faces."

Their ancestor was a close relative of *Psittacosaurus,* meaning "parrot lizard." This small dinosaur walked partly on hind legs. Its name came from its parrotlike beak. The creature probably used this to cut off tough leaves. Tough-leaved flowering plants thrived in Mongolia where *Psittacosaurus* roamed. That was more than 100 million years ago.

Protoceratops worked its great jaws by powerful muscles anchored to its bony head crest. Some of its descendants had crests guarding most of the back. Some had horns above the nose and eyes.

A Triceratops charges a Tyrannosaurus. The three-horned dinosaur was heavier than a bull elephant. It was as long as three small cars. Even the fiercest enemy would have been wary of its long horns.

After the "parrot lizard" came dinosaurs that walked on all fours. These were *Protoceratops* or "first horned face." They had bumps above the eyes. The back of their skull grew into a bony crest.

In North America over the next 35 million years, 18 kinds of horned dinosaurs appeared. The largest was *Triceratops* or "three-horned face." *Torosaurus* had the longest crest. Its skull was longer than that of any other land animal. *Torosaurus* was also one of the last of all the dinosaurs.

After the Dinosaurs

About 65 million years ago the dinosaurs and most other large beasts suddenly died off. Why they died remains a mystery.

Dinosaurs may have vanished due to disease or eating poisonous plants. But why did sea reptiles also vanish? Some people believe that poisonous gases from volcanoes caused their extinction.

Deadly particles from an exploding star may have been a cause. Dust that darkened the sky may have occurred when a huge meteorite hit the Earth.

The big animals, most likely, were killed by cold weather. The world was slowly cooling down. Severe climatic changes occurred as the continents drifted apart. Cold-blooded dinosaurs were too large to escape winter frosts by hiding in holes.

Even if the dinosaurs were warm-blooded, they didn't have hair. Their bodies would have lost heat quickly as the air around grew chilly.

When dinosaurs vanished, birds and mammals became masters of the land.

Fossil Dinosaurs

Scientists study fossils to find out information about dinosaurs. Fossils are the remains of animals or plants that have been preserved in rock.

Dead animals protected from decay form fossils. Decay is prevented when a corpse is quickly covered up by substances that shut out air.

Evidence shows that some dinosaurs were killed and buried by the shifting sands of sandstorms. Others drowned in floods and sank in mud that settled on the bottom of a lake or river.

Soft parts of dead dinosaurs usually rotted quickly. Bones and teeth decayed last. They would be dissolved by water. Sometimes minerals in the water would filter into the holes left by decaying bone. Hard minerals, like iron phosphates or silica, replaced whole bones.

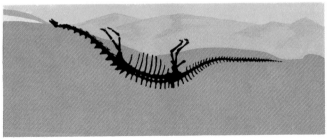

Five pictures show how a dinosaur fossil is formed.
1. *A drowned sauropod sinks to the bed of a lake.*
2. *Mud settles on the lake bed and buries the body.*
3. *The flesh rots and minerals partly turn the bones to stone. The sand and mud above harden into rock.*
4. *Earth movements raise the rock and fossil dinosaur.*
5. *Weather wears away rock and exposes the fossil.*

The bones were turned to stone or "petrified." Meanwhile, the mud or sand around the fossil bones turned to rock.

Millions of years later, the Earth's surface may have moved the fossil-bearing rock above ground. Next, the top layers of rock wore away by frost, rain, and rivers. The fossils showed up on the surface.

A palaeontologist exposes huge bones, embedded in solid rock, in Utah's Dinosaur National Monument. Visitors can see carnosaur, sauropod, and other fossils in the gallery.

Left: The American palaeontologist, Othniel Charles Marsh, helped to discover more kinds of fossil dinosaurs than anyone else. In the late 1800s his fossil hunters found 19 kinds.

Right: Edward Drinker Cope helped find nine new kinds of dinosaurs. Cope and Marsh disliked each other. Their teams of fossil hunters were rivals.

Fossils are sometimes found by chance by miners and road builders as they work. Others are discovered by palaeontologists. These are scientists who study fossils.

Fossil hunters search in places where rain, rivers, or workers have uncovered rocks that were made in the Mesozoic Era. The likeliest rock layers contain ancient sand dunes, lake mud, or sandbars that once blocked rivers.

Fossil hunters look for pieces of fossil washed out of the rocks. These pieces may lead to a fossil dinosaur still stuck firmly in the rocks.

Removing a brittle fossil can take months. A team of fossil hunters may start by using picks. They work carefully with trowels, chisels, and brushes to free fragile fossils from rock.

Treating the Fossils

Digging up a fossil dinosaur is just the start. The fossil hunters harden crumbly bones. They use a special spray. They wrap layers of thin, soft paper around the bones. Then the bones are cushioned with special bandages or foam. Fossil hunters must then take the fossils to a museum. Experts can study them in workshops and laboratories.

Inside a museum, workers remove the packing. Technicians may spend months trimming off stone around the fossils. Their tools include hammers, chisels, and even dentists' drills. Engraving tools and needles remove the last unwanted specks of rock.

Once fossil bones are clean, palaeontologists try to fit the bones together. Technicians then rebuild the whole skeleton. Metal struts and clamps are used to join the fossil bones.

A palaeontologist wraps up fragile fossil bones to prevent them from breaking as they travel to a museum.

The fossil dinosaur is ready for display after years of work. Palaeontologists will study its bones. Its skull shows what kind of brain, eyes, nose, and teeth the creature had. These clues help experts discover how well a dinosaur could think, see, and smell, and what kind of food it ate.

Leg bones show if it walked or ran. Some bones have marks on them made by muscles. This hints at the shapes and sizes of those muscles.

These studies help scientists to know what dinosaurs looked like and how they lived.

A skilled technician uses a small drill (below right) to remove particles of rock on a fossil bone. Tools like this can vibrate at 30,000 times each second. Sandblasting may be used to free a fossil still stuck in a rock. The rock will be blasted with a jet of air containing sand. This wears away the rock.

To erect a fossil dinosaur skeleton, experts use metal rods and clamps as props. The props are placed so that visitors who gaze upon the bones scarcely see them.

Dinosaur Mysteries

Fossils do not tell us everything that we would like to know about the dinosaurs. For instance, we will never know which dinosaurs left certain footprints. And we can only guess that dinosaurs were brown or green to match the earth. This "camouflage" would have helped to hide them from enemies.

We know that dinosaurs laid eggs. We often do not know which dinosaur laid which eggs. We also do not know whether dinosaurs cared for their newly-hatched young or left them to fend for themselves.

What Really Were Dinosaurs?

Experts differ about what kind of creatures dinosaurs actually were. All believe that most dinosaurs had long leg bones and stood upright. But animals like these today can run fast and far. Could dinosaurs do that? Scientists disagree. Some say dinosaurs were cold-blooded reptiles. They only had enough energy to run in short bursts, like the lizards we know today.

Other scientists argue that dinosaur bones show that the beasts had a rich blood supply to power their muscles. So dinosaurs may have been warm-blooded or half way between cold and warm.

People used to think of dinosaurs as reptiles. But maybe they deserve their own special place in the animal kingdom.

Above: Fossil baby Protoceratops that died hatching. We do not know for certain if Protoceratops' parents looked after their young. But baby Hadrosaurs found in one nest seem to have eaten food brought by the parents.

Below: Fossil footprints like human hand prints earned an unknown reptile the name Cheirotherium or "mammal hand." Later, scientists found fossils of its relative, the sauropods' ancestor Ticinosuchus.

Index

The animals pictured on the title page of this book are, from left to right, Brachiosaurus, Iguanodon, Tyrannosaurus, Stegosaurus, and Triceratops.